BREDOW

Phoebe Monk

Thank you, Shmuli, for encouraging me
to finally sit down and write this book.

Bibliographische Information der Deutschen Nationalbibliothek: Die Deutsche Nationalbibliothek verzeichnet diese Publikation in der Deutschen Nationalbibliographie; detaillierte bibliographische Daten sind im Internet über dnb.dnb.de abrufbar.
© 2025 Phoebe Monk
Publisher: BoD · Books on Demand GmbH, Überseering 33, 22297 Hamburg, bod@bod.de
Print: Libri Plureos GmbH, Friedensallee 273, 22763 Hamburg
ISBN: 978-3-8192-4854-2

Prologue

To be honest, I was not really interested in history lessons during my school period. All those events seemed theoretical and far away. Besides, I knew most of the countries, that were discussed in our lessons, only from hearsay. German history was also presented in a way that we peers could not really relate. Mind you, I am talking about the Eighties.

However, all this changed overnight, when I - now in my fourties - discovered the manuscripts of a certain Robert Bredow. I held a large pile of old, paled paper in my hands and had trouble to decipher some of the words. But the more I read, the more interesting the content became. Bredow had been a professional soldier and a post office clerk. Later on, he became the deputy of the head of the Hamburg prison and the director of the remand prison. All of a sudden, history transformed into a real and tangible matter to me. It was incredible to read about life in prison, the means that the National Socialists came up with to maintain their demand of power and the sheer number of mostly harmless people that were denounced and beheaded.

When I came up with the idea of a book, I wanted to make sure that every detail, that can be found in Bredow's script which he wrote for the history research center in Hamburg in the early fifties, was correct.

I looked up all the names, all mentioned events, checked the dates and numbers and read other books (including the texts about the Hitler times published by the prison itself) and double-checked everything once more. All was true. Unfortunately, I should add, given the cruel circumstances.

Subsequently, I contemplated on how to transform all the material concerning Bredow into a book.

Firstly, I skipped parts of his personal view, whenever I figured that it was irrelevant or repeated too many times. I had shortened passages and corrected expressions and grammar occasionally trying not to alter Bredow's writing style too much. And I have deliberately put the focus on the horror of the executions and the criminal conduct of the Gestapo. In doing so, I want to counteract the trivialisation of the Nazi period.

Doubtlessly, that would be in Bredow's interest.

Sorry about the not-always-correct English. I had a hard time, translating the old German sayings, the special military and judiciary terms. If you find errors, please forgive me.

Oh, and there is a lot of cursing and sarcasm. I left it in. It would not have been authentic, if I had omitted or replaced it.

But now, let us hear what Bredow himself has to say:

* * * * * * *

When the history research center in Hamburg asked me to provide my recollections concerning the Hitler years (especially those during my work period), I was more than willing to comply.

I would like to emphasize that my aversion was not directed towards the National Socialistic Party in its original form. In this Party, I saw the only chance to restore the monarchy. Furthermore, it made good sense as a counterweight against the Bolshevist danger. My hostility emerged on the grounds of the circumstances that the National Socialism, when rising to power, became the Nazism. This Nazism contained an abhorrent viciousness and created a violation of human rights that we have never seen before. With my manuscript, I would also like to express that authorities, administration and judiciary made it far too easy for the Nazi regime. There had always been political oppositeness, but it is only of use, if it is in compliance with preservation of human rights, rationality and justice.

After the upheaval in the year 1933, the then-president of the penal institution in Hamburg, Christian Koch, was relieved of duty and forced to retire by the Nazi regime. His position was turned over to State Councillor and Gauinspektor of the NSDAP, Max Lahts. Upon application of Lahts, I was assigned to direct the remand prison (which was the second biggest of this kind in Germany).

With the beginning of the Nazi regime, a "purge" regarding all authorities was implemented, in order to remove all politically unreliable elements. This purge primarily included KPD and SPD members (the communists and socialists). I was assigned to supervise the purge, which suited me fine, since I was now able to reduce the menacing disaster at least a little.

Some dismissals had already been carried out before I started my new duty, but I was determined to put that to an end. From now on, no officials should be dismissed on political grounds or be confronted with disadvantages. My aim was to keep my loyal and devoted personnel out of all political movements and hostilities. Luckily, State Councillor Lahts was tolerant enough not to interfere.

Jewish officials had to be dismissed all the same. On demand of the State Administration of Justice, I was supposed to write a proposal in order to dismiss the competent Jewish Chief physician of our military hospital, Dr. Cohn. At first, I was able to prevent that, but soon enough, some Party and SA members refused to be examined by Dr. Cohn. Eventually, he immigrated to America, which was probably a clever move, since nobody could possibly anticipate what fate would have awaited him in the hell of the Nazi regime.

Once the Nazis came to power, the number of prisoners rose dramatically. Consequently, auxiliary staff was needed and that came from the Party, the SS and the SA. At that point, the denunciation got completely out of control. They criticised, they snooped around and they reported. The one thing they did not do was work. Seasoned, professional officials were insulted and spoken of as "Santa Clauses" whose positions should be taken over. There were no more than 20% that were doing their duties humbly and decently. The rest of the staff was useless and a heavy burden for me.

As stupid as they were – they were anything but harmless. They were the reason why the main characters were allowed to carry out their horrible devilries. That also included the security guards at the concentration camps.

I was obliged to pursue all those reports. However, I was able to secretly file them away. Naturally, that was a very dangerous act, since the informers realized soon enough, that nothing was happening or following upon their reports. If those reports had gone through, the people, that were mentioned in them, would have been handed over to the Gestapo. My dangerous deeds boomeranged back to me in form of a massive agitation by the Party some years later.

I would like to give an example to demonstrate how easy and malicious those denunciations were:

An SA member reported a constable, claiming that he had severely insulted the Party and the Führer. Albeit, the SA member had this information from a third party. I stepped in immediately, since the constable would be in grave danger if this affair was transferred to the Gestapo. Several hearings later, it turned out that the whole thing was a fake.

I used cases like this one, to start a big fuss and to put the craving for denunciation in perspective. It did stop for a while – but not due to understanding. Simply due to fear.

It was a lot easier to avert reports that came in from members of other Parties. For instance: There was a company secretary who had been accused of having insulted the Party and Hitler in a delicatessen store. I ordered the accused over to my office, but already simmered the affair down, before he had even spoken a word. The man had not expected this goodwill and started crying. He had always been a democrat, he said, and his longterm friend, that had denounced him, was a member of the Socialist Party. I ordered to be put through to the man on the phone and reproached him with his friendship to the accused and his membership of the Socialist Party. I demanded that he dropped the charges or I would let him be snatched away by the officials. The man backpedalled immediately: He admitted that he did not hear exactly what the accused had said. Finally, I released the accused and recommended that, from now on, he should be more cautious about who he befriends.

But it became even nastier: An employee of the penal institution (member of the Socialist Party) accused the predecessor of Lahts, State Councillor Koch, of a commission crime. I looked into the file of this employee and realized that the man owed many thanks to the now accused.
During interrogation it turned out that his accusations were completely groundless and far-fetched. Ich reckoned that the man felt uneasy since he was a Socialist and tried to prove his loyalty. I wrote a request to dismiss him and to cut his pension and both requests were affirmed.
This man did not at all fullfill the ethical or the character suitability for his position and profession. He was lucky that this report of his never went underway. At present, chances are high that he would be in prison for that.

The denunciations were not limited to Party members but spread like a mental desease among the whole country. Even among prisoners, who probably hoped to improve their situation by reporting others. Whenever possible, I nipped this in the bud.

Aside from the fact that I had my problem with the German greeting "Heil Hitler", it made a good example for the constant denunciations:

The already mentioned Dr. Cohn, who had been close to his retirement, had some problems with his hearing and eyesight. However, regarding his profession, he was extremely competent and, above all, very popular. It so happened that he would not respond to the greetings, simply because he did not hear it! I had to step in regularly, in order to keep him out of trouble and harm. The German greeting became a scale for political conviction.

Yes, in those days there was not much strength of character around and that was a major misfortune. Otherwise, the horrible things that happened soon after, might never have happened at all.

With the rise of the Nazi tyranny, the number of prisoners rose simultaneously. Not due to more crimes, but due to the reason that more Communist members and more Jews were imprisoned. Up to then, the number of Jews in prison was the smallest compared to other groups. Now it was the other way round. Strangely enough, Jews that were ready to leave the country immediately, were dismissed at once. But only in the beginning of the Nazi period. I remember well the case of a Jew, whose arm had been broken by the Gestapo during interrogation. He was allowed to emigrate. Just another example for the stupidity of the regime: This man would, once abroad, show his crooked arm and tell everyone in detail about his experience with the Gestapo.

From now on, living with a Jew was regarded as a criminal offense. Before, nobody cared about that. The reports, filed by so-called Aryan women who had sexual contacts with male Jews, were outstandingly disgusting. It was very easy for those hideous creatures to blackmail the Jews afterwards. But strictly speaking, the law, that supported this rascality was even more hideous than the deed itself.

During the war, it was ordered that Jewish prisoners should not receive meat any more. But with a trick that my senior cook came up with, we circled around this perfidy:

The meat was thoroughly cooked and the meals for the Jews were prepared with the now incurred broth.

After the surge of power in 1933, the Communists were the first to receive the "blessings" of the "Third Reich". The Gestapo and the Kommando z.b.V. were busy arresting anyone and anything conspicious or any person that had been tipped off by inmates. In Hamburg, political prisoners were either brought to Camp Wittmoor, in an empty wing of the Fuhlsbüttel prison, or to our remand prison, at least in the beginning. Camp Wittmoor was harmless, compared to Fuhlsbüttel, where the security guards consisted of auxiliary police officers belonging to the SA, Marine-SA and SS. When some of those prisoners were transferred to our remand prison for their judicial sentencing, I heard of many physical abuses. The state justice administration was not able to interfere, since those deliquants were not judiciary, but protective custody prisoners and they had no right of disposal. Nevertheless, I was of the opinion, that we could not tolerate these incidents and came up with an idea, which led to the fact that 150 prisoners were transferred to the wing in the Fuhlsbüttel prison. The reason was, that we had the authoritive power on that property and could counteract any violent clashes that arose. It was a big venture, but even though it was successful, I gradually became one of the most-hated men by the Gestapo.

The mix-up of remand and police prisoners is already absurd under normal circumstances, but with the political change in 1933, the Gestapo transferred huge numbers of political prisoners to the police station, which was located in the basement of our remand prison. In a wink of an eye, we were faced with extreme overcrowding. The rule said, that police prisoners had to be brought before the examining magistrate within 24 hours. He then decides whether the prisoner has to stay in remand or is to be set free. Obviously, this rule did not seem to apply to the Gestapo and therefore, I had a lot of serious trouble until I was able to restore the former regulations with the help of the Hamburg State Office.
In our remand prison, I urged my officers to have a very close look concerning maltreatings of prisoners. That was not really necessary though, since the Gestapo snatched prisoners over to their city house. And even if the returning prisoners did not open their mouths, it was very obvious what had happened to them.

I ordered them over to our military hospital and made sure that they could stay there as long as possible. However, without the help of my loyal doctors, this plan would never have worked.

I remember one certain prisoner, whose buttocks had literally been beaten away. Using an excuse, I lured those, who were responsible for this deed, over to our prison and showed them the terrible wounds. Not much impressed, even when threatened with a prosecution, they left the prison.

On the contrary: They threatened me and the professor in charge to take us away as well. That was how powerful the Gestapo already was. There was nothing they had to fear. The coward acts of violence on behalf of the Gestapo constantly increased – though the concentration camps did not even exist yet. Countless times, I had to simmer down, prevent or elude such evil deeds, always having in mind that my own life was at stake. And as if that was not enough, the denunciations among our own personnel came on top of that. The mental burden I suffered became unbearable.

I would like to enlarge a little upon the Kommando z.b.V. (*Z.b.V. stands for "for special use" – author's comment.*)

This notorious Kommando consisted of policemen in uniform plus a police captain. That captain invited us over one day to have a look at their "business" in the Hamburg street Große Bleichen. So we went. The present policemen were literally surpassing each other in telling us about their "heroic acts", which were the cruelties they implemented to squeeze out confessions from their prisoners. Later, on trial, those confessions were often weakened or completely revoked. The "interrogation chamber" was a naked room, but what caught our eyes were the leather whips and the long rods placed in the corner. There were dark stains on the walls that turned out to be blood. All I had heard so far about the inhumane incidents referring to the Kommando z.b.V. corresponded with the truth.

This Kommando, that was subordinated to the Führer, who once said: "We will fight for the soul of all workers, up to the last one", thinks that whips and torture are the necessary measures? That fact alone shows how insane and felonious this man always has been.

In summer of the year 1933, the previous protection camps have been substituted with concentration camps. Within the prison in Hamburg Fuhlsbüttel, they chose the wing for the women. SA Brigade Leader Paul Ellerhusen had been appointed the leader of this new camp. I was afraid of a significant deterioration of the situation concerning the prisoners, but Ellerhusen played it down, with the words, that he certainly knew how to treat these people. Oh well, he did prove that, did he not, with the result that he himself went into prison for 12 years after Germany was freed. (*He was prematurely released – author's comment.*)

The minute the camps were put into operation, the first abuses came to the surface. Some of these badly wounded inmates were transferred to our central military hospital, since they were in urgent need of medical care. Unfortunately, I could not find out, what had been done to them. The fear was too big, to be exposed to even worse abuse as a consequence for talking, and I could very much understand that. So, the minimum I could do was to keep them in the hospital for as long as possible (and even longer), to avoid that more harm was done. Four months after the camp was established, my path crossed again Ellerhusen's.

I told him about the severe abuses and realized, while talking to him, that he was well aware of the things that were going on in the camp. That fact finally led to his long imprisonment.
The lust to torture and the increasing power frenzy of the Gestapo was not only felt by criminals, but also by homosexuals, stock market swindlers and decent citizens, who had dared to criticize the political developments, merely out of patriotic concern, and had been reported for speaking their minds.

At the beginning of 1934 (before the Röhm affair, in any case) I had to deal with prisoners that came in from a camp near Stettin. They were witnesses in an upcoming trial. Before their departure back to the camp, one of them spoke of the terrible tortures that took place there. I tried to make all those prisoners talk, but they feared for their lives, so they would not say a single word. When I promised them that they will stay under my care until the affair is cleared up, they started talking. What I then heard was simply unbelievable.

Among other things, they were forced to stand at a wall, presumely to be shot to death. They were shot at – with blanks! Then they got whipped. My report about this matter was passed all the way up to the Minister of the Interior (at that time Hermann Göring). Over the following days, I did not hear anything about this matter and assumed that my report, like most others, was secretly filed away. However, two weeks later, I was informed that there had been a thorough sweep throughout the camp.

Some prison sentences were spoken on grounds of the abuses, and Göring himself had presumely flown over and ordered the shootings of several SS security guards. It is a shame, that this procedure was not carried out in other camps as well. As soon as Heinrich Himmler took over the command of the German police, more prevention-, education- and killing-camps cropped up.

The beating and torturing continued and the responsibility lay with the camp leaders. In the Zirbes-trial, the main accused, namely Robert Zirbes, stated that they did not receive the pizzles just to look at. With this statement, he doubtlessly confirmed that Ellerhusen did not only know what was going on, but also concurred. But it was not only him. His second-in-command, Willi Dusenschön, was a first-class tormentor, who took part in the cruelties himself.

(*Due to statute of limitation, Dusenschön could not be sentenced for his crimes later on. Author's comment.*)

You probably wonder why so little of these cruelties in the camps went public at that time. Even local groups or areal leaders of the NSDAP did not seem to suspect anything, or rather, they thought that I was spreading evil rumours whenever I hinted the truth. The German people really did not know anything then, and that is an important fact, since the Allies misjudged the situation later. The released inmates would not talk, since they feared the worst, if they opened their mouths about the ongoings in the camps.

And even if something went public, it was mingled with so many lies that the real nastinesses were regarded as negligible. That was not at all in the interest of the prisoners.

A radio station from Straßburg once spread the news that women were put in bath tubs and scalded with hot water in our remand prison.

I was asked by the Reich Crime Office to make a statement regarding this report. I announced that nothing of that sort had ever happened or will happen, since I would counteract any violent deeds with the full rigour of the law. Besides, if a situation like that had taken place, I would have known it.

Naturally, on hearing this, the Schadenfreude on behalf of the Gestapo was immense, but that did not stop me from continuing to report any abuse that happened in the camps. Soon enough, the camps established their own sick bays, and the transfers to our prison stopped. That was very unfortunate. At least, on our premises, the prisoners received a bit of humanity. Only when Hitler was due to pay a visit to Hamburg, the abuses and the transfers over to us increased considerably – presumely as a precaution against possible assassination attempts.

There was Hitler, being driven through the streets with masses of people cheering from left and from right, oblivious to the fact that other people were brutally whipped and beaten for their "Messiah".

And even if they had no means to know what was really going on, I can still not understand how people were so uncritical regarding his attitude and happily became his slaves. Given that open criticism was not possible, it would nonetheless have suited them to be more reserved.

I am of the opinion, that this insane glorification led to the circumstance that Hitler became the worst oppressor. With the aid of the Gestapo, he had started a war against his own people. Ordinary citizens were no longer safe against deprivation of rights and being dishonored, no matter how small or trivial the offence had been.

A good example for this is the story of a merchant, who was put into a camp for stock market swindling and afterwards transfered to me. The man was a mental wreck and shivering all over. I had difficulties to elicit what had happened to him. After the cruelties that had been done to him in the camp, he regarded his stay with us as heaven, he sobbed. Now that told something, I would say. His report about the ordinary cruel deeds was no news to me, unfortunately. After the year 1945, I had often been asked why we, as the judiciary, did not intervene with those offences.

Well, some of us would gladly have done so, but the constitutional state was virtually no longer existent, and the judiciary was like a ghost in the shadows.

I was talking with chief public prosecutor Dr. Drescher and president Lahts about the case where a prisoner in a camp had been shot down on an "attempt to escape". That was plain murder, since the yard in which the prisoner happened to be was surrounded by high walls, that made any escape completely impossible. I urged Dr. Drescher to look into this matter, which he obviously did. A few days later, some prosecution officials entered the camp for investigation. The result was, that they were thrown out with the words, that, if they ever tried again to make another appearance, they would be kept right there.

However, I was fortunate to meet some bold judges, and I am convinced that the majority of them had rejecting thoughts about the Nazism. Here and there, more civic courage would have helped to put things straight. The fear and insecurity made the Nazism as exorbitant as it finally had become.

In the times when the concentration camps were first established, occasionally some reports appeared in the newspapers whenever prisoners were shot dead for resistance.

The number of murdered people rose, but there were no reactions. Consequently, the murdering continued uninhibitedly, until it reached the level of mass murdering by gasifying, hanging and the lots. Especially regarding the Jews, the increase of numbers was considerable. It was all too easy for the Nazism to proceed like this, and I was pretty alone with my view and position. But that would not stop me: I kept prisoners that had been abused and were sent over, and I made clear to the Gestapo that I would not hand them back again. I threatened that I would use this method for every single prisoner that showed traces of abuse. Soon enough, the abuses stopped. That was an unmistakable proof, that the Gestapo was uneasy whenever confronted with a firm opinion. Those bandits mainly thrived on fear and terror.

Another example for the fact that it was quite possible to stand up against the Gestapo was the Pulvermann case.

This half-Jewish merchant from Hamburg was handed over to me from a camp in the year 1941. He had been a competition horserider and owned a large estate between Kiel and Rendsburg. He had been the president of a German-American trade company. The copy of a letter, which he had sent from Oslo and that contained some captious phrases, had led to serious consequences for him. His trial was soon to take place, but meanwhile I was told that he was supposed to return to the camp, should he be acquitted. I ordered to disguise him as fatally ill, which he firstly did not understand until I explained what was in stock for him. On trial, he was sentenced to half a year prison time, but that was already satisfied with the time he stayed with us in the remand prison. He was free to go. And the minute the verdict was announced, two men from the Gestapo appeared to take him away. I, of course, would not have any of this. But the matter became rather delicate: The Gestapo did not believe at all, that Pulvermann was sick. They threatened to send over their own SS-doctors and investigate the Pulvermann case among others. The whole thing, they said, was obviously a trick and they would not allow to be deceived by me any longer. I screamed at the officers via telephone that I would send their SS-doctors flying out and that I am in command here and not the Gestapo. Then I smashed down the receiver.

At least I was able to protect Pulvermann nearly two years in the remand prison. In October in the year 1943, I was relieved of all duties. On the same day, Pulvermann was taken away by the Gestapo and 4 weeks later, he was dead. Presumely cardiac arrest.

Prisoners, that had been sentenced to preventive detention on trial, were in a better position. They stayed under the judiciary system and were safe from being killed. In this context, I remember the case of two young men aged around 20. They had been sentenced to 4 years imprisonment, since they had had homosexual intercourse with another man, without being homosexual themselves. They just wanted to blackmail the poor lad. The verdict was absolutely correct for that deed, but I was astounded by the request for preventive detention, which I firstly rejected. The prosecution, however, asked me to reconsider my view, since those men would very likely be transferred to a concentration camp after their prison sentence.

I understood and changed my opinion, which led to an astonishment on behalf of the chairman of the Criminal Court. I told him my reasoning in favor of the two men. This, among other cases, clearly shows how difficult the situation back then had been for the judiciary.

In order to explain the then present circumstances in more detail, I would like to describe the nationalsocialistic idea and its ideology. Until the famous power surge, the NSDAP worked with a certain social program. Even if idealistically bound, it was at least a program, which was accepted by the majority and which condemmned everything that had been existing so far. After the power surge, instead of implementing the promised freedom, a massive deprivation of rights and tyranny cropped up. Everybody wanted things to get better, but nobody said how this could be established. The people did not even know what had been promised to them. The same could be said about the ideology: It was a slogan, but nobody knew what it really meant. Alfred Rosenberg, the original father of the NS-ideology, had tried to give the matter some substance by writing his book "Myth of the 20th century", but miserably failed.

The very essence of the whole book seemed to be that he wanted higher and cultural perceptions such as belief in God and ethics, to be concentrated on the person of the Führer. Whether he really meant it this way or another, has never satisfactorily been determined.
But do not think that the Nazis have not done anything for their ideology: There were the so-called Gauleader Schools, where courses were held. A certain number of employees from companies and public authorities had to attend such a course where, among other things, they had to learn how to tidy a room properly. As if they woud not be able to do this without such a ridiculous course! When the director of the Lübeck prison told me that he had been ordered to attend a course, I immediately forbade it.
I wondered why the Nazis were so anti-Communist, since all what they did, would have filled any Communist with pride. Depersonalize and make everyone part of a mass with the effects visible up to today.

The Nazi Party had declared this attitude even before their seizure of power: "Mass is nothing. Mass is uncritical and unscrupulous. Mass has to be led."

And that was far more than blank theory: Apart from their own people, everything was mass to them. That was the fabulous ideology.

Speaking of ideology, I remember the day when we had a staff meeting with 250 employees present, during which I asked some officials, who had just been back from a course at the Gauleader School, to tell us something about the ideology. Nobody said a word. I tried to motivate them to say anything at all, but they just stared at their feet. I told them that it is okay, since I do not understand the nationalsocialistic ideology myself, but I would have an ideology for them as a substitute: 1) be decent 2) be decent 3) be decent. That is national *and* social.

It did not take long until I got reported for this statement. I was accused of mocking the ideology. The same ideology that even the denouncers did not understand and that did not at all exist.

I was regularly exposed to spying and denouncing anyway. During a speech, that I held to the staff at the prison in Hamburg-Fuhlsbüttel, I complained about the leakages of information concerning some auxiliary civil servants. Furthermore, I pointed out that most of my trouble was caused by Party members among the staff and that I preferred fair acting and thinking over arrogance and pomposity. A decent person is decent, no matter how long he or she was a member of the Party.

Naturally, that was reported as well, and the Party asked me whether I had said those words or not, which I affirmed. I even took it a step further by saying, that I assumed that the Party was thinking the same, otherwise I would be in the wrong place. For a long time afterwards, I did not hear a thing, but that was illusory. They were trying to bring me down and were waiting for a good opportunity. But for the moment, they could not do anything about it, since I had exactly said what the Party, originally being nationalsocialistic, had publicized itself!

Since there seemed to be no direct way to knock me down, they started to stage a hideous agitation against me, and this is how they did it:

In the Fuhlsbüttel institution, there had been an auxiliary security guard with the name Engel, who had been a long-term Party member. He had slept through his night vigil and was consequently dismissed. However, not by me, but by president Max Lahts. Engel went to the Party Court and applied for proceedings against himself, since he regarded himself as unfairly dismissed. Actually, a case like this should be brought in front of the Labour Court and not the Party Court. So it was clear enough, that some officials in the Party were using this man as a medium, in order to carefully stay in the background. And the incredible outcome was this: Engel took legal action against *me,* and not against Lahts. The whole affair was artificially inflated and 70 witnesses had to testify. Those, supporting me, were snarled at. Those, being against me, had to testify under oath, but without the knowledge of the local Court Chairman. President Lahts did not budge at all, concerning this affair, which I thought was rather treacherous of him.

In the meantime, I had more than enough of this monkey show and asked the local Gau Judge to end this nonsense. But nobody wanted to interfere with the proceedings, and when the main trial was announced, I had been summoned as a witness.

The whole room was decorated with Nazi flags. In the background there had been a rifle range with several rifles. At the head end, there was an elevated tribune, also decorated with flag tissue. And there, the Party Court was enthroned, in full uniform and with pistols at their belts.

This so-called main trial started in the evening and went on all night long. When I entered the room first, I was already enraged at was I saw, and I asked who actually belonged to the Court and what all the other people were doing in here. There was a lot more dispute between me and those arrogant snobs as the trial went on, and about three o`clock in the morning I offered the Party Judge a good spanking. Since I was a chairman of a Party Court myself, my behaviour was reported to the Gau Direction, the Gau Court and the Supreme Party Court. The chairman of the latter, a ridiculous clown named Lösche, wanted my expulsion from the Party. Now I stroke back: I wrote a letter to the Supreme Party Judge, Major Walter Buch, told him about the whole farce and asked him to find out who was behind this conniving machination.

I wanted to initiate legal proceedings against all those backers. I was fully aware of the fact, that now they would even harder try to fry me. And the revenge appeared, as a 33-paged indictment against my persona. All those lies and twists that were listed there, were completely absurd. It was more than obvious, what mischief could be conjured up when incapable Party Judges have the right to take oaths from witnesses.

In this indictment, it was written that I

1. was the most brutal director throughout Hamburg

2. had protected Socialdemocrats and Democrats in my staff, whereas I had misbehaved towards and dismissed Party members.

3. I had damaged the reputation of the Party in my speeches held in front of my staff.

4. had forbidden the "German greeting" (True! But only on the pit latrine and as long as the military greeting was in order for uniformed civil servants)

5. did not pursue reported Party opponents in my staff.

6. never wore a uniform as a Party Judge (true! Never had one.)

7. have never attended Party meetings. (True!)

8. have mocked the nationalsocialistic ideology.

9. have regarded Party membership as secondary and called Party members rascals (only if they really deserved it).

10. have never shown a Swastika, only the marine war flag (I have never owned a Swastika).

11. have said, concerning the Heil-Hitler-greeting: Imagine, the man's name had been Meier, by any chance. (That had been overheard by a secretary – an obediant Party member! - of president Lahts)

12. have beaten two political leaders, who had appeared in my appartment for collecting donations, and had arrested them for four weeks (big lie – I will come back to this later).

13. was an opponent to the movement according to my speeches (absolutely, especially in the way they saw this movement)

14. have shown unfair behaviour regarding the dismissal of the injured-by-war and Party member Engel.

The list went on and on, with all the lies of these snobs, these "more than 100% Party members", to whom it did not matter what kind of damage they conjured up with their urge of denunciation and ruthlessness. It was in fact those "little Nazis", that beat up people in the streets if they did not greet the flags with an upheld hand. That was the outrageous arrogance of that Party.
The Party that once preached: No human is like another, but who came thick and fast with enforced conformity!

Now back to my indictment: Allegedly, I hit and put two political leaders into prison for four weeks, but the story was a completely different one.

I had been told that some young lads were roaming the streets in Hamburg and were terrorizing citizens. They insulted by-passers and collected money for the Party, so they claimed, but instead, they blew it. One fine day, my daughter was complaining, that she and her girlfriends had been badmouthed by two political leaders, due to the fact that they did not greet. Unfortunately, there was nothing I could do about it, since I had no knowledge about their identities. Late afternoon, the same day, I was home alone and chilling on the couch, when the doorbell rang.

Expecting the postman, I opened the door. It was those lads, insisting, that my daughter was supposed to greet them. Now those two came just about the right time. I let them in and offered them to sit down. I took a seat close to my library, where I had hidden a loaded pistol. It did not take long for a serious dispute to evolve.

Those lads were about to take out their guns, but I had mine already pulled out with the words: "Hands up or I will shoot." The police was summoned and the two arrested.

Next morning, the police departement called to ask whether I wanted to institute criminal proceedings against them, which I declined. Instead, I ordered them over to our remand prison, where I was ready to take some action in my own style. Those lads had excused themselves with the claim, that they did not know who I was. Which, of course, meant that they could do just anything they want with anybody else. I asked the policemen why they did not interfere with affairs like these, and I got the obvious answer: Nobody knew what they were at any more and nobody would want to have trouble with the Party. There you go: Everyone was trying to avoid trouble, and the Party and its uniform have become holy terms. But that did not apply to me: When the lads appeared in my office, I sent them flying across the room with a good smack.
Then I told them that I would keep them under arrest in our premises for four weeks for terrorizing the people. Unseen to the two men, I told one of my officers to show them one of our shabbiest cell and then bring them back here. When they returned, the big Party heroes had diminished to small whimps, that begged me with tears in their eyes not to lock them away. I dismissed them with the words, that if I hear just once that they were at the people again, I would put them away – not for four, but for eight weeks.
I never heard of them again. Logically, I excluded them from the Party. Actually, they should be thankful for that after all, thinking of the denazification some years later.
At any rate, the ridiculous Party Court exaggerated enormously, concerning my behaviour towards those snobs.

In 1940, the Führer Chancellery issued a serious reprimand about this affair that happened in 1933 (signed by Reich Minister Martin Bormann), claiming that I had heavily damaged the reputation of the Party, by slapping political leaders. Well, I am rather of the opinion that if I had not slapped them, I would have damaged the reputation of the Party a lot more, since otherwise, they might have become brutal sadists or murderers.

It was somehow strange, that the Führer Chancellery also dealt with the Engel affair. What sort of cross connections were there between the Chancellery and the Hamburg Party? This brings me to another story:

It was in 1937, when we had a woman in our remand prison for communistic activities. One day, a high-ranked Party Officer appeared and requested to hand the woman over to him. He had appeared without a visit permit, so I ordered to reject him.

The following day, the man reappeared and requested to talk to the woman who turned out to be his sister. Impressed by his uniform, my security guards did not dare to say or do anything wrong, so they begged me to come. The man's behaviour was pretty rude, so I threw him out. He left under a wave of curses and threats. Two days later, he appeared again, but was stopped at the gate. Due to his inappropriate manners, I prohibited his entry.

Simultaneously, I informed the leader of the Führer Chancellery (at that time Reich Leader Philipp Bouhler) about the disgraceful behaviour of one of his men. Shortly after, my main security guard, who was present at the first confrontation between this man and his sister, was ordered to Berlin. And then, all of a sudden, he was dead …

Whether this high-ranked officer had told a wild story about the events or whether he had complained in a way, that officials finally had found some means to take me down: It does not matter which. It was one way or another the typical perfidy which belonged so much to the Nazism. And soon enough, the hunt for me was initiated, which resulted in the already mentioned 33-paged indictment.

On grounds of all those accusations, the political leading forces had to do something against me. However, I knew that this was impossible as long as there was an official legal proceeding going on in the same matter. Therefore, I applied for investigation proceedings against myself. During the interrogation on behalf of the prosecutor, I finally heard in total of the accusations against my person.

It turned out that all the witnesses were forced to give evidence against me. Their oaths were quickly taken, so that they could not revoke anything afterwards.

Unfortunate for me, the prosecutor was a Party member as well, otherwise it would have been easy for me to find out who was behind the whole conspiracy. The whole investigation took about six months and then, finally, the resolution said: The collected accusations were partly untrue, partly torn out of the context. This resolution was submitted to all relevant Party Offices, including the Führer Chancellery. It went quiet for a while, but the agitation has caused serious damage to my person and the relationship to president Lahts cooled remarkably, since he had done nothing to support me in any way, shape or form.

All of a sudden, big surprise: I was promoted to Senior Civil Servant. Though the agitation against my person was not even over yet. I had absolutely no explanation for this – I only knew that General Prosecutor Dr. Drescher had asked the Party Court whether any proceedings were planned against me or whether any sort of concerns were existent against my potential promotion. That did not seem to be the case, and I strongly believe that the decision to promote me was passed around the Führer Chancellery which would have flown off the handle, had they known.

When my promotion went public, the wave of agitation rose again, but Dr. Drescher was able to keep further trouble away from me. I am still extremely thankful to him, since – due to my disputes with the Party – I was in life danger many times, and without his help, I would not have gotten out of some situations in one piece.

Given my strong dislike concerning the Party, one must wonder, why I had become a Party member in the first place. I would like to explain that.

It was in the year 1931, when I was asked one fine day to hold a speech about the colonies. I needed a colonial world map for the speech and paid a lending fee of three Marks for it. At the end of my speech, I was about to collect the money when someone suggested to use that money as my first monthly contribution for the Party. That was not what I had in mind, but I only shrugged my shoulders. At that time, I regarded the Party as a sort of stepstone to restore the monarchy. The Party itself did not mean anything to me. I was solely concerned about the nation and the decency of the state leadership.

Long before he ever came into power, I named Hitler a mischief-maker, but back then, I did not anticipate what reign of terror he would bring onto the German people with the support of his Party.

So, finally, I became an arch enemy of the Nazism, and I still cannot grasp why and how the people could indulge themselves in such a personality cult, and would not refrain from it, even when the complete deprivation of rights surfaced.

If, at all, there was a somewhat logical explanation for this development, we have to look at the situation of the country after the First World War. 1918, when the war was lost, the German Empire was destroyed and substituted with the Weimar Republic. The aversion towards the new Regime was massive, and throughout the whole country, small battle associations arose. They would have been quite successful, if there had been more solidarity and less individualism among them.

It was only in 1923 when there was a merger under the title „United patriotic battle association" (*in German: Vereinigte vaterländische Kampfverbände, author's comment*) with Erich Ludendorff at the lead. So far, a nationalsocialistic movement had only been existing in Bavaria, and the new revolution was supposed to start from right there, with Hitler as political and Ludendorff as military leader.

However, the planned march to Berlin was cancelled (and the government in Berlin therefore rescued), since there had been some discrepancies between Hitler and the Bavarian government). Hitler, of course, did not let this pass, and at the famous beer hall meeting in Munich on the 8th of November 2023, he had several Bavarian officials arrested.

Hitler entered the tribune, shot in the ceiling and declared the Berlin government as deposed. To order the march to Berlin, he had to release those arrested government people, who allegedly concurred with the movement now.

Once free, they gave their orders. But not for the march, but for an attack on Hitler and his battle association. Towards next morning, when the two opposing forces clashed at the *Feldherrenhalle* (General Hall), several people got shot and wounded which resulted in 16 dead people just on Hitler's side and an overall total of about 20 casualties.

The Beer Hall Putsch was history and consequently one less concern for the Berlin government.

In the now following trial, Ludendorff was acquitted, and Hitler received a penalty of about 5 year prison time, but did not serve even one year. He was kept in the prison of Landsberg, and the circumstances under which he had been imprisoned, were so mild that he was even able to write his book "My battle" right there. During his stay, he was transformed into a hero, and that is how the cult about his person and the rise of the nationalsocialism were initiated.

After being released, Hitler was subject to a speech ban, however, the aversion towards the government was so immense, that he did not care and his Party grew nonetheless.

The German people was confronted with seven million unemployed and a rising, threatening communist danger. So, the nationalsocialism was regarded as the minor evil.

When the speech ban was over, Hitler flew from one city to another and spoke nonstop. And the tormented people cheered. It is quite disgraceful, that the responsible statesmen did not take this development seriously. It would have been their duty, to erase both the communism and the nationalsocialism in time. I remember having come across one of those Hitler visits in Hamburg. The hall was packed to the brim; there were people collapsing continuously, who were pulled out of the hall by SA-men like cattle. When Hitler belately entered the hall, a tumult and hail-shouting started that I thought these people were like a hord of possessed. Disgusted, I left the hall to get myself a cognac in a pub across the road. I was completely fed up and swore myself never to attend another Hitler meeting. And it had been the only one.

Naturally, the devilish deeds by Hitler were only possible on grounds of the blank trust. On the other hand, it would be too easy to speak of a general collective guilt. Whoever thinks that way, has not fully understood what happened in those days. This overboarding cult has to be seen in direct connection with the political and economical breakdown and the rising threat of the communism. I am very sure that nearly all individuals, who cheered for Hitler back then, did not suspect this reign of terror and they are, after all, the very ones that have been deceived.

Another example for the helplessness and weakness of the government prior to the Hitler Regime: One day, I was attending a speech by Goebbels, in which he literally said: "We will be elected by the Constitution, but afterwards, whatever we do with the Constitution, is solely our own affair." Right there and then, Goebbels should have been arrested and the Party prohibited.

But they were helpless cowards, and therefore, the government has the main guilt as to the development of the events.

Back to the procedures in the penal institution. When I had another round of discussion with president Lahts about the dreadful outrages in the concentration camp, Lahts pulled Reich Govenor Karl Kaufmann into the affair and effected the removal of "Commander" Ellerhusen. Not only in this context has Kaufmann shown some decent behaviour: In our institution, some of the officers had not joined the Party, and there was an interest to secretly find out what the reasons were. The answers were nearly always the same: They had not joined any Party whatsoever and wanted to keep it that way. Lahts was of the opinion that something should be done about that, however, Kaufmann told him that being a member of the Party is in no way mandatory and there should be absolutely no enforcing. I must say, that I appreciated his attitude. Unfortunately, not all administation offices saw it likewise.

Whether it was Göring or Himmler, I cannot say for sure, but now – instead of the arbitrary abuses - they officially established the death sentence. They had started with stick beatings for minor offences, which were ordered by the camp director, who pompously called himself "Commander" and usually was an uneducated person. Especially the official touch of this torture made this degradation something beyond comprehension. This was not about an actual punishment. This was about satisfying pervert genetic disposition.

An ex-camp prisoner told me that the director of the women's camp in Ravensbrück (*about 100 kms north of Berlin, author's comment*) was an affectionate and caring family guy, but the minute he arrived at the camp in the mornings, some women were put onto the whipping rack, who he personally "worked on".

In its frenzy for power, the regime rampaged against its own nation. All the prisons and concentration camps, with their torture chambers, their killing and prevention camps, were overcrowded. The whole Germany was like one big prison institution, and, according to the incarnated devil Goebbels that was the "freest and best democracy in the world."

Prison sentences had lost their former meaning completely. Now, it could just happen to anybody and logically, the real culprits benefitted from it. But they did not submerge, instead they roamed about as allegedly politically damaged people.

I remember the case where a man with multiple criminal records became a police director, and he was not the only one.

With the following examples, I would like to point out how easy it was back then to be sentenced to prison:

A so far respectable, good-natured man had been sentenced to four weeks prison time, because he had – just for fun – pinned an allegedly found Party badge on himself.

A master locksmith was sentenced to one year prison time for talking to some friends about the Röhm affair in a bar, plus, he had said that it was terrible that the Führer was allowed to order executions to an unlimited degree without any official court hearing. A prison officer had overheard this and the man was taken to the police station. I saw to it that the locksmith got the odd leave so that he could continue managing his business. Then I took care of the informer. It turned out that he was a kind of marriage-impostor, so it took little effort to sentence him to four years imprisonment. The exclusion from the Party, which I also arranged, hit him hard. And again, the old saying was still true: "The biggest evil throughout the nation, was and is denunciation."

There were plenty of examples like the ones I wrote down, and it showed that even the most harmless citizen was no longer save.

You may want to condemn whatever laws came with the Nazi regime. However, there was one law that could have been debated: It was implemented for sterilisation in order to prevent offspring with genetic deseases, as well as severe or repetitive sexual offences.

Most of the persons concerned even gave their aproval, since it was an easy and harmless surgery, generally carried out in our military hospital in the remand prison. Naturally, abuse had to be avoided, but that had never been the case at us anyway. I would have heard of that.

It was a different story with the emasculations of sex offenders. That was quite a complicated operation which never met the expectancies. The emasculation was already a part of the verdict on the trial proceedings and therefore a part of the penalty.

The basic thought behind this was to completely alter the mindset of the criminal and to stop his sex drive. The success was moderate, therefore, shortly after, there was the odd criminal being brought back to our prison. Occasionally, health complications (mostly of mental nature) could be seen after the surgery; even deaths occurred. And since the emasculation, also according to doctors, was no guaranteed instrument to render a sex offender harmless, those surgeries slowly faded out. Well, science had been quite mistaken about their original prognosis. That was most unfortunate, since many sex offenders told me personally that they would have wanted such a promising surgery, to get rid of their disastrous sex drives, under which they mentally suffered a lifetime. What a humane tragedy!

Speaking of humane tragedies, I would like to illustrate the significance of the death sentence, which was not always necessarily related to the regime. I will put my focus on the executions in our remand prison. Unfortunately, those death verdicts were also a result of the then existing zeitgeist.

I do regret that very much indeed, since it will damage the image of the judiciary for a long time to come. It had adapted itself way too much to the will of those sadistic ruling powers. Maybe to satisfy them in order to prevent worse things, but personally, I believe that a good deal of individual courage would have been in order instead. Here are a few examples, how the judiciary followed the zeitgeist in those days:

Case 1: A Polish woman, working in a fish factory, had an argument with her forewoman. The latter was of the opinion that the Polish woman had spent too much time in the restroom.

During their tussle, the Polish woman hit her forewoman on the head with her clog, resulting in a bruise and a headache. The Polish woman was sentenced to death.

Case 2: A young Pole, working on a farm, was told to watch over a small boy. The boy started screaming, and it was noticed that the Pole handled the genitals of the boy. The Pole was sentenced to death.

I have read about a case, in which it was pointed out, that servants used to behave in this manner in order to sooth children. Maybe the Pole had been raised with a similar custom? On the way to the place of execution, he constantly wailed: "Head off for this, head off for this." It was an accusation to the whole mankind.

Case 3: A Pole had an argument with his employer, who was a farmer. The farmer threatened him with a club. The Pole also grabbed a club to defent himself. It never came to physical violence – still, the Pole was sentenced to death.

Case 4: A Pole and a German girl *(the girl was under special care, which is usually the case when parents cannot cope anymore for whatever reasons, author's comment)* were working on a farm together. She lifted her skirt to squeeze some pimples on her thigh. The Pole touched her naked thigh. He was sentenced to death.

Case 5: A Pole, who urgently needed to urinate, was chased by some young girls. He desparately tried to shoo them away. The girls encouraged him to show them his genital. To get rid of them, he did so. He was sentenced to death.

In fact, the penalty for Poles, when sexually interacting with German females, was death sentence. However, that was never the case in the above described examples!

Another story to show the typical zeitgeist is the story that involved a post officer who had been sentenced to death as a "violent criminal." Now this caused a huge wave of outrage among the civil servants.

I took a closer look at the case – the accused was, after all, occupying a cell in our remand prison. I would describe him as decent, objective and not at all plaintive, though the threat of the death sentence hung over him. A year passed before his attorney was able to enforce a new hearing, which – due to my reports and my conversations with the man – I had to attend as a witness.

Regional Court Director Kreiss passed the only sensible sentence: 2 years imprisonment. One year had already been served in our remand prison, and the remaining year was put on probation. The man was released immediately. We would have needed more judges like Dr. Kreiss. It is more than unfortunate, that he had been so badly skinned and salted, during the denazification process.

It is rather unlikely to gain a precise picture of the many executions in our remand prison without the relevant files. I had written a brief, but thorough report about every execution, but nearly all of those valuable reports regretably were destroyed during capitulation. Reports of this kind were not mandatory, however, I believed that, as the director of such an institution, I owed it to procedures like these. My reports would have been an important contribution for the awareness on how decadent the Hitler era had been.

My reports contained all the aspects worth knowing, for instance: ID, date of conviction, which court spoke the verdict, summary of the crime, execution date and who announced it, oral reaction of the offender, how did the offender behave in the death cell, what did he say, request or write (I took copies of the letters), what and how much did he eat and smoke, how did he behave when brought to the place of execution, how many seconds from handing him over to the executioner to the fall of the head, who was the prosecutor in charge, what happened to the corpse, who received the inheritance of the executed.

Whenever an execution was appointed for the next morning, I did not sleep the night before. I was at odds with God and the whole world and over and over again I asked myself: Does it really have to be like this? Is there no other way? There were plenty of cases for which the death penalty was not appropriate, for instance, executions on political grounds.

On the other hand, there were criminals, who had killed cowardly, maliciously and brutally and to whom the lives of others were worth nothing at all.

Seeing those, I always came to the conclusion that it had to be, if we did not want to be part of the guilt, of the murders and violent crimes. That was our duty and simultaneously our tragedy.

According to official regulations, I had to be present at every execution. Nearly all of the convicted begged for mercy, except the political convicts. As brutal as the murderer behaves towards his victim, as dear is his own life to himself. Getting a lifetime imprisonment gives them the hope for getting released, may that be due to political changes, war or escape.
We have already seen that anything is possible at any moment. It was our duty to enforce scruples by roughness and violence onto those people owning a killing nature. Especially among our youth, the number of murders rose dramatically. I do have a vast understanding and indulgence for some derailments of our youngsters, but certainly not for clever, beastly murders that had been committed without an obvious need. Our youth does not want pity, they want responsibility, liability and, above all, justice.

Some crimes committed by young persons, however, cannot be assessed according to law and atonement. I remember the case involving a 15-year-old boy, who committed an unbelievingly brutal sex crime on an 11-year-old girl in a forest in the district of Hamburg. The deed was obviously planned, since the boy had equipped himself with a sharp knife and ambushed the girl on her way home. When he was brought to the remand prison, I saw a child with soft facial features, and we were left to wonder how anything like this could be possible. He was sentenced to death.
In the morning, around 90 minutes prior to the execution, he started getting quite restless. He asked whether it was true, that the convicted was allowed one final wish. He would desire a girl for the last time. Now this is a moment where you just do not know what to say and you ask yourself why a young human being is condemned to live with such a terrible sex drive.

A drive so enormous that it would not even silence in the face of death. Strictly speaking, it is not the boy's fault. It is a wicked game of nature or the devil.

How can you see where the beginning or the end of a guilt is? On one hand, they say: "Whoever spills human blood, their blood shall be spilled as well." On the other hand: "Do not judge, so that you will not be judged yourself." What is right and what is wrong? Evil, mental conflicts are rising within oneself, but in the long run, I come to the conclusion that it was out of the question that this boy would get away with this alive. He would have been a constant danger, even behind bars.

The death sentence was annulled in the Weimar Republic era, but partially re-introduced during the Papen government. It was only with the beginning of the Nazi regime that it was generally established once more and extended to other crimes that had nothing to do with murder. Typcal for the new regime was the lack of the even smallest sense of justice, as well as its seeking for revenge and its spitefulness directed at political opponents.

In the beginning of the 1933 re-established death sentence, the executions had been carried out with the guillotine, which had rested until then in the museum of our remand prison. The platform, onto which the convict had to climb 9 steps up, was remarkable and served the circumstance that the spectators could entirely "enjoy" the whole procedure. The convict was strapped onto a kind of stretcher. Above his head, about three meters above the ground, there was the slide bar with the guillotine. Under the head of the convict hung a long sack which extruded far into the empty space below. When the guillotine was engaged by a downhanging rope, the head flew – with a considerable swing – into the sack.

When there were more than just one execution, the sack was exchanged, to make sure that the next one in line would not see this terrible scene. Yes, even in the Nazi era, they showed some respect....

Not only the assembling and dismantling of the guillotine caused difficulties, also the height of the device, since it protruded well above the prison walls, meaning, it was visible from outside and was declared as disturbing. In Prussia, the ax was the common device for executions, so it was agreed to introduce this method in Hamburg as well.

The executioner was above the moon about this idea, and, with professional pride, he declared that he personally disliked the guillotine a great deal, since, with the ax, he could work a lot "neater". Oh yes, he was a sensitive and emotional man, that executioner was, and I was constantly amazed how firmly he hit his target with the heavy ax, when he swung it. The guillotine was history, once and for all, and it went back to its old place in the museum. Mind you, it was nearly 60 years old, and there was a certain danger, that - when the guillotine swooshed down - the whole apparatus would collapse.

In that case, the executioner and his three henchmen, together with the corpse of the conduct, would have fallen into the depth below. Well, in that case, my pity would have had its limits, since those guys disgusted me a lot, due to the fact that they thought their jobs were something holy.

Shortly after the Nazi regime took over, I noticed that an executioner and his assisting men wore Swastika wristbands. Enraged, I ordered them to take those off. That hit them really hard, which showed once more how much the Nazi mania had infiltrated the masses already.

In days of yore, the executioners received 750 Marks for every execution. Back then, this luxury could have been afforded, since executions were very rare. During the Nazi era, this compensation was slowly reduced. The latest regulation set the compensation to 40 Marks for the first execution and 30 Marks for each of the following. Furthermore, travel expenses were refunded. Despite this new regulation, the executioners earned a lot more money in total now. I came across an executioner who had carried out more than 50 executions in Silesia. With this statement, he did not win my sympathy. From the outside, the man gave the impression of a modest craftsman. However, what was most striking, were his dead eyes.

The first executions primarily involved political opponents. During the following years, those executions considerably ebbed down. Their focus now lay on murders, incurable repeat offenders, and the odd "racial shamers". Heads did rarely come off due to political reasons. However, with the beginning of the war, the executions reached a level, that we had never seen before.

It was no longer about the communists or similar political opponents. Now, literally over night, it was all about crimes dealing with danger of collusions, crimes using an air raid situation, serious economy crimes, so-called antisocial parasites, car trappers, pacifists in connection with undermining the army, pacifist comments, relatives of people that had been expelled from the army, Poles (even for minor deeds) and so forth. In our remand prison we had about 45 - 50 death candidates every day now. The death sentence was declared if you just said that the war could not be won, even if it had been said simply out of national concern. That also included relatives of recruits. The number of deserters rose with the ongoing of the war. Our remand outpost in Hamburg-Altona had to give up half of its space and turn it into an army prison. In there, among others, were soldiers, awaiting the death sentence. In former wars, shootings were not the norm, due to a verdict from the War Court. So here was the zeitgeist as well, and the methods of the Gestapo swashed into the army, as the following incident shows:

We received a soldier with a death sentence who was supposed to be shackled at all times. A reason for this, such as high danger or suicidial tendencies, was not mentioned. The whole instruction was submitted in such a rude manner, that I promptly picked up the phone to get connected with the Senior War Court Govenor. He was not available, but I told the office clearly, that in my remand prison, nobody gets shackled if I do not see a good reason for it. As an old professional front soldier, I knew well enough that you cannot win a war with Gestapo methods and numerous death sentences.

Any sort of punishment had always been big fashion in the army, even in former times. I recall an experience from my own life:

After I had been leading a machine-gun formation over several years, the commanding general wanted to have a look at the punishment books. He found out that I had ordered no punishment within the last two years. He wondered how that could be possible: An excellent led troop section that functioned without any punishment? Surely there must be something wrong!?

With this example, I would like to point out, that this was not new at all. Anything should be accomplished with punishment. The harsher, the better. In the Nazi era, that meant terrible rascality, of course.

Now back to the marine soldier with the death sentence. I found out that he had broken eight shackles in that prison in Altona. When I visited the man in his cell, I ordered to take away the shackles and asked him, what this was all about. He told me, that he had been hung up so high, that he could barely touch the ground with his toes. He could not last long like this, so he broke the shackles one by one. There we had another evidence that the tortures of the Gestapo and the camps had their influence here all the same. And when this strong man broke his shackles they all went chicken.

I gave him a bright, sunny cell and promised him that – if he behaved well – the treatment will be likewise. Never ever had there been complaints about this man.

What a perfect example for the amount of guilt the Nazi regime loaded upon itself, with all its incapability, arrogance and lust for torture. I would like to tell another story in this context, though it has nothing to do with the executions.

One day, I received 40 Polish officers from a war captivity camp, that were accused of undermining the German military forces. It was completely beyond me, how they should have done that. All possible ranks were among them, even a senior judge, and most of them spoke excellent German. I reminded them to obey our regulations, but they protested and wanted to be treated according to Geneva Conventions.

Very directly, I told them that the only rules they had to obey were our prison rules and that was final. Eventually, I visited them in their cells and had a chat, for which they were grateful.

Then came the day when I was visiting one of them who had suffered from insomnia, resulting in me organizing a sleeping pill, and now I asked him how he had slept, when a sergeant, who happened to overhear this, lost his temper. That takes the biscuit, he snarled, asking those bastards how they had slept. Nothing of that sort would ever happen in the camp, he barked! There, they would have been treated differently. When I was alone with the sergeant, I ripped him to pieces. Consequently, he became quite subdued and meekly replied that those guys were indeed different back at the camps. "The way you treat them, that seems the only logical outcome," I snapped.

The recipe is simple: Let people choose between a good and a bad treatment. Normally, they will choose the good treatment with the return service of an appropriate behaviour on their behalf.

After a while, I was told to inform the Poles that the proceedings against them were stopped. I asked them if there was anything else I could do for them. They conversed among themselves, then told me, that they would like to heartily thank me for the good treatment. They had had the opportunity, so they continued, to convince themselves that the horror stories about German prisons were one big lie. The moment they reached their hometurf, they would put this straight.

I did not comment on this. I just thought:

It could have been that way …

As already mentioned, in the years 1933 and 1934 mostly political opponents were beheaded. It was such a pity about those bold men, which were betraying themselves with a fake idea – just like the pretended ideology from the Nazis. At the same time, Nazis, that had been sentenced by the former government or were still in remand prison, were suddenly set free. That was the new justice: Immorality and decay. Like nothing else, they wanted to exert revenge on political opponents, and with this attitude, they created martyrs. Even on their way to the place of execution, many of them shouted communist slogans, before they lost their heads.

Never will I forget the unique story of a certain Mister Sander. He allegedly had stabbed a policeman. His execution was set for six o'clock next morning.

During the night, around four o'clock, I received a call informing me that the lawyer of Mister Sander had put in a request for a new hearing. Sander, so it seemed, had been forced to confess due to torture on behalf of the Gestapo. At present, he withdrew his confession, so, together with president Lahts, I drove over quickly. Time was running out.

Sander was already awaiting his execution with a cut-off collar and shackled wrists, so that – if the request was rejected – he could be executed on time.

The hastily summoned jury was debating for a very long time and one might imagine what horrors Sander lived through during his wait. Even president Lahts was a nervous wreck, chain-smoked and had one coffee after the next to calm himself down. The verdict was spoken around eight o'clock. The execution was called-off. Lahts gave Sander his own breakfast, two glasses of cognac and a cigar. But this verdict was only temporary and Lahts had to jump in once more. He achieved that the verdict was turned into a 15-year imprisonment.

President Lahts did have a soft spot. I noticed that, during the executions he attended, he frantically looked in another direction and closed both eyes when the guillotine came down. Then he would leave the place in a hurry.

If I describe Lahts so humane, I do this for reasons of justice. We had several quarrels nonetheless, due to his emphasis on the entitlement to power, regarding the Party. As a civil servant, I strongly disliked this and many times I foiled his intentions.

In early days, it was common to let twelve witnesses from bourgeois circles attend an execution. But soon, there were far more than those twelve, because not only the prosecution, also the Gestapo printed attendence permits. When things got out of hand, the whole witness rubbish came to a halt. The lust for sensation was unbelievable. The minute an execution was announced, our telephone would not stop ringing. Later, there were no more public announcements, and that was a relief. Plenty of people have to be present anyway: prosecutor with his secretary: makes two. Executioners with three assistants: makes four. Doctor and paramedic: makes two. One lawyer, one clergyman.

A chief inspector and eight officers, in total nine and one prison director. All these alone were twenty people! Reich Govenor Kaufmann never attended an execution, very contrary to police president Wilhelm Boltz, who desperately wanted to attend the execution of escapee Hannack. Even before the execution took place, Boltz and I had a serious dispute. Right before the execution, there was a loud turmoil in the administrative section of our building.

I went over to see what was going on, when I encountered Boltz, who was badmouthing my officers. He wanted to attend the execution, but the doors would not open. I told him, that he should have been on time, since those doors have a special security lock and cannot be opened easily afterwards. Without uttering another word, he stomped on, through the now open doors, hurrying to the place of execution. Mind you, that man was our police president!

I would like to give you a more detailed view on the case involving this man called Hannack:

Initially, he had been convicted to 15 years of imprisonment. He managed to escape several times. Last time from the highly-secured prison in Oslebshausen near Bremen. As a cat burglar, he was very agile, but he was a friendly chap nonetheless. Together with another criminal, Adolf Petersen, called "The Lord of Barmbek" (*Barmbek is a district in the North of Hamburg, author's comment*), he was on the rampage in Hamburg for a certain period of time. Petersen, however, betrayed him. Whenever Hannack was up to something, Petersen would rat him out to the police and receive payment by both sides. When Hannack was caught once again, due to Petersen's betrayal, he was transferred to our prison. I started talking to him, when I had to explain why he had to be shackled when being in the yard for his daily walk: There was nobody who knew the soft spots of the prison like he did, which he outrightly admitted. From that moment on, I regularly sat together with him in his cell and we had nice conversations.

Due to Hannack's interrogations, Petersen was finally caught and sent over to us. For Petersen, the situation was hopeless: He would never get out again.

One day, Petersen asked me to switch off the night light (which we keep on for surveillance especially for serious offenders and potentially suicidal ones), because, he claimed, he could not wind down. I permitted it and two days later, he hung himself.

Unfortunately, things were not looking good for Hannack either. During the Nazi era, the shooting at a police officer was followed by death sentence, even if – in Hannack's case, who shot while escaping – nobody was shot dead.

In the night before the execution (I was home and on my way to bed), I received a call from the prison: Hannack had begged to talk to me one final time. Well, what should I do; I dressed and drove over. It was nothing in particular that Hannack told me, just some bits from his personal life. Furthermore, he stressed that he never had had the intention to shoot anybody dead. On the contrary: He had always shot in a way that he gained sufficient time for his escape. If he had wanted to kill someone, he would have been able to do so, he added. I believed him. It is a pity that, by law, a case like his ended up in a death sentence. We were just smoking a cigar, when president Lahts suddenly appeared on the scene. He had heard that I was with Hannack. Lahts listened to Hannack's story and afterwards, we left together. Lahts was a nervous wreck again, since a death sentence had been spoken though nobody got seriously hurt. He needed a cognac, he said, to get his senses together. We went to a pub and had a few grogs. However, those drinks had no effect on Lahts and he decided spontaneously to ask Reich Govenor Kaufmann to pardon Hannack. So we went over to see Kaufmann, but he refused the sudden request. The affair was in the hand of fate now, and I was only home for about an hour, before I had to appear in the office again. I then did the only thing that I could do: Secretly, I let Hannack receive some whine and cognac.

Shortly after, Hannack appeared on the place of execution in a merry spirit. He greeted everyone present with a joyful: "Good morning, Sirs", then his head came off.

Naturally, this whine and cognac thing was against regulations, but that would not stop me to do it time and again. But, due to all those informers, I had to be extremely careful. And regulations or not: I hope that the Lord will forgive me.

Not only with Hannack, also with Fritz "Fiete" Schulz did I have some very interesting conversations. Fiete had been sentenced to death some months ago, but the execution papers had not arrived yet. He told me that this waiting was inhumane terror for him and I must agree with him. He winced whenever a key was put into the lock. This would not happen in Russia, he explained. There, when it was believed that a person had to be done away with, the procedure would follow without hesitation, instead of months of torture.

It seemed that he was okay with the fact that he had to be eliminated. We did discuss political issues quite often, since he not only enjoyed that, but it gave him strength, as he said so himself. Not long after, the execution papers arrived and he was executed on the 6th June 1935. On the place of execution he shouted: "Long live communism" - then it was over.

On 4th November 1936, the communist leader Etkar André was executed. At the beginning, I would not really warm up to him, because he had something cold and lurking about his persona. But during his last night, we did get a bit closer. It was a rough night anyway. There were loads of policemen around our prison, since communist riots had to be expected. When I visited André in his death cell, he was busy with wolfing down tons of delicacies. And he would not stop ordering more, much to the dismay of our cook, who was therefore obliged to be at the stove all night. I was fascinated by the nerves (and stomach) of André, with whom I started an interesting conversation. He told me that he had been treated quite well in our remand prison, whereas in the concentration camp, he had been whipped. He also showed me some photographs, among those was his wife, for whom he had cared and who was now in Paris.

Etkar André had put in requests for a new proceeding, but without success. The last refusal came in the morning about four o'clock. Around six, he was led to the place of execution. He greeted me, then he shouted loudly: "Down with Hitler, the mass murderer!"

That was how this man died, who loved life and would not fear death.

On 15th December 1942, SS-Standartenführer and Gauhauptamtsleiter Wilhelm Jankowsky was executed. He had been the leader of a food rescue formation, that was engaged whenever a calamity broke out. Such a big desaster faced the city of Lübeck, when it was the victim of a heavy air raid. The retaliation came pronto: the english city of Bath was severly damaged. Meanwhile, the food platoon was on its way to Lübeck, but the city was able to take care of itself. Consequently, Jankowsky and his personnel treated themselves: They ate only the best, they drank and smoked. And you could not call Jankowsky stingy: Lübeck's high officials and high-ranked party members were also invited, including the mayor, who – when the affair went public – shot himself. On the evening before his execution, Jankowsky said to me: "While they drove off with about 200 corpses above our heads, we were sitting in a traditional cellar restaurant below and poured down twenty-year-old wine." Logically, the wine had also been stolen from the food platoon.

Shortly after Lübeck, a similar attack hit the city of Rostock, which led to the necessity ordering the food platoon over. And that led to a similar orgy. On its return to Lübeck (to scoop up the deposited food), many goods disappeared. Hitler was not at all amused, when it came to the theft of goods. His newly invented regulation led to serious punishments on behalf of the thieves. Jankowsky and his men got caught. He and two other leaders were sentenced to death. When the men were deported at Lübeck's main station, there was a huge public resonance. The rioting people would not miss for their lives to finally be entitled to badmouth party officials as much as they liked. The two other leaders had a stroke of luck: Their death sentences were transformed into prison time. On the evening prior to his execution, I visited Jankowsky in his cell. He was looking at photographs of his wife and children. Tears shimmered in his eyes. We chatted a little and bitterly he complained how cowardly and evil many of his kind eluded punishment. People that had profited from the whole affair but now loaded the entire guilt on him. I asked him whether he had ever thought about the fact, that this regime had covered the whole German people in so much disaster and how cheap and worthless a human life has become. Things look indeed different when you, as an SS-Standartenführer, feel Hitler's newly implemented harshness on your own body.

Yes, he responded, he had thought about that himself, but his insight came too late. He went on, explaining that those orgies took place quite regularly and even higher ranks than his were involved. Nobody ever gave it a second thought. As an example, he told me about his encouter with the Gauleader of Schleswig-Holstein, Lohse. Lohse had motivated him to take part in an excessive boozing binge, and the booze was standard among the party anyway.

Even the famous SS-leader Erich Hilgenfeldt had ordered parcels from him, of course via his wife, since he himself wanted to stay in the background. Later, Hilgenfeldt claimed that he had known nothing about those parcels and that his wife must have acted independantly.

Many times have I talked with those that faced death sentence and it was an extrem mental burden for me. However, I did it nonetheless to ease their last hours. It was those political prisoners that I really liked, since I could well anticipate their disgust concerning the regime. We did not get many political prisoners though; most of them were convicted and executed by the People's Court in Berlin. With the title "The last hours", Count Alexander Stenbock-Fermor had written down the memories of the clergyman Harald Poelchau, who was working in Tegel, in Plötzensee (both in Berlin) and in Görden (which is a district in the city of Brandenburg). When reading Poelchau's descriptions, the big differences between Hamburg and Berlin are strikingly obvious, regarding the handling of the prisoners before and during the executions.

According to Poelchau, 2032 prisoners in Görden and 1800 in Plötzensee have allegedly been executed up to the year 1944. That would be 6-7 times the number of those in Hamburg. And the year 1945 has not been documented at all, neither in Hamburg nor in Berlin. The disrespect for humanity, that must have taken place there, is beyond imagination. If I have said that judiciary was straight on its way to follow the regime and the SS, I can only add: It was in the very middle of it. Poelchau calls those executions judiciary murders, and that is exactly what they were!

Poelchau describes that certain prisoners had to wait days before their execution in the death cells with their hands shackled. They even had to write their last letters with tied hands. We have never ever done this in Hamburg, it was never necessary. Only when the prisoners were taken to the place of execution, their hands would be tied and that was inevitable. Poelchau continues by illustrating how the executioner and his henchmen visited prisoners in their death cells to pry into their mouths for gold teeth, that they could crack out after the execution.

Another thing that I would never have permitted in our prison. Additionally, it was strictly forbidden for executioners to enter the death cells.

As to Poelchau, one of the worst things he recalled were those nights of the 7th, 8th and 9th of September in 1943. In Plötzensee, there were about 400 criminals with a death sentence. Shortly before, the prison was heavily damaged due to an air raid. The Reich's Ministry of Justice had instructed that those men should be "put to death" as soon as possible. And exactly this happened in the following three nights – without any advance notice to them, so they could not even write their last letters. In groups of eight they were brought into the "execution shed". They had to stand on a stool and they were hung onto iron hooks with a noose. Then the stool underneath was pushed aside. They had to hang like this for twenty minutes to make sure they were definitely dead. Then the next eight prisoners were brought in. It would be interesting to know who was responsible for this shameful judiciary act and what sort of consequences they faced. The Reich Justice Minister Dr. Thierack committed suicide in 1946. It is a pity that he was not hung onto one of his iron hooks.

The participants in the General Putsch from 20th July 1944 were also meant to end their lives on those hooks. Poelchau wrote that, for some of them, the "slow death" had been ordered by Hitler himself. Those deliquents were more carefully hung, so that they would only be dead after a longer torture. Additionally, rumor had it that Hitler ordered that the whole procedure was filmed until the last twitch of each victim. Especially the officers were meant to be humiliated in a special way. They had to dress in prisoner cardigans and trousers.

General Field Marshall Von Witzleben had to hold his trousers up with his hands, because they were way too big for him and kept dropping to his feet. Those that were hung here in such an evil manner were precious humans with their only crime being resistant to a devilish, inhumane regime! They were artists, scientists, workmen, clergymen, scholars, teachers, officers, high-ranked officials et cetera, that were transferred to the hands of the executioners.

They were a thousand times more precious than those that did nothing at all, due to the fear that they might face "inconveniences".

Poelchau continues his report with the story of the executed Karlrobert Kreiten, whose father had received an invoice about 639 reichsmarks and 20 pfennigs. He did not get any other message. I am at a loss for words concerning this depravity.

Kreiten was one of those 186 people that were hung from the gallows in those fatal nights in Plötzensee.

During the calamity after the 28th of July 1943 (*air raids of the Allies, author's comment*), there were nearly fifty criminals with a death sentence in our remand prison. Already during those terrible days, it was ordered to execute a large amount of them. I immediately protested against that, with the justification that I could not expect my officers to face such a mental burden in the middle of Hamburg's inferno. Besides, due to the gradually increasing water shortage, it would be impossible to wash away all that blood, plus, the corpses would not be taken away under the given circumstances. As a consequence, the prison Dreibergen near Bützow was picked as the place of execution and it was ordered to take the prisoners there. That was not at all what I wanted, since, with my appeal, I had hoped to save some of the prisoners. I had a strong feeling that the regime would finally break down anytime soon.

Reluctantly, I had to hand over the convicted, but in all the chaos that occurred, nobody noticed that I secretly kept four clergymen, to whom I will get back later.

From July 1943 on, there were no more executions in Hamburg. They were re-introduced in 1944, but I do not know any details, since I had been relieved of duty in October 1943.

After the successes in the first war period the party, and at its head that raffish Göbbels, boasted that those successes had only been possible due to their "education". But when the first drawbacks were felt, it allegedly was the sabotage on behalf of the generals that was responsible. As if those generals would saw off the twig on which they sat. Anybody with a normal brain could comprehend that this statement was completely illogical. It was those drawbacks that slowly caused a mistrust concerning Hitler's infallibility. However, there were always those others, that would not or could not recognize that the regime itself was one big deception. Some people insisted on believing in the Führer, no matter what.

The odd rejection would worm itself out via captious jokes, but those could be seen as insidious and would be punished with the concentration camp. I remember an evening being on my way to Hamburg's main train station, when the air raid sirens went on. Entering the nearest shelter, I encountered a familiar Gestapo officer, whom I would describe as moderate. A merry, tipsy group of people were keeping us company. They were joking about the government. When the Gestapo officer rose to intervene, I pulled him down at his sleeves, begging him to leave those people alone. He slowly sat down again. That group had no idea how close they were to being handed over to a camp. This joking around was evidence enough for what the German people really thought by now. Simultaneously, the regime, with its brutal methods, made quite clear how insecure it had become. So, inevitably, it all came down to the final fatality.

In spite of the terrible days in July 1943, the people could be put off for a while, with the fairytale of the nearing retaliation, which would turn around the war in our favour and bring victory. Whoever did not believe this and said so loudly, made an acquaintance with the guillotine.

For our remand prison, those days were a nightmare as well. Just technically speaking the accomodation for 1,700 - 1,800 prisoners in protective areas was simply not possible. The few small shelters, that we had, were for the administration personnel and for important files. Whenever the air raid went off, the prisoners would get restless. There was even an instruction by the Ministry that serious criminals and those with a death sentence should be shackled when the alarm started. But I would not obey.

I even opened the doors to the yards, and thank God this dangerous and risky gamble had no consequences. We did not get bombshelled during my time. That happened later, when I had already been forced to retire.

We hardly had any water during those dark days, since the fire engines needed enormous amounts. Our cells were overcrowded, the toilets blocked.

The prisoners helped themselves by throwing their excrements out of the window into the yard below. A thick layer of dust covered it all.

It was a miracle that no epidemic broke out, with the stifling heat we were facing at the same time.

In the middle of all this chaos, we received a demolition squad of fourty men (all had been concentration camp prisoners), who were supposed to tear down walls and blow duds. They were decent and precious men and I enjoyed looking after them. Often, in the evenings, when they returned to the prison, they carried wounded or dead comrades on their shoulders, which was no surprise at all, regarding the dangerous work they were doing. The corpses lay in our cellar and the stench was so unbearable, that I urged the police to take them away. Well, they did so, but only carried them right up to the front of the gates. There, they lay beside the city trench. The police did not have enough vehicles at their disposal to remove all the corpses.

In order to ease the situation in the prison a little, I suggested to the General Prosecutor that we put those on leave that had committed harmless crimes and who will not expect serious punishment. Five prosecutors arrived to check the files of the inmates.

The files were not much help, so they decided to interrogate the prisoners which, of course, led to formidable lying. My concern grew and I planned to make my own decisions concerning the dubious cases.

Shortly after, when I returned from my lunch break, I saw a group of prisoners around the front gates. Among those were some, that I had combed out as being unsuitable for a leave. It turned out that, during my absence, there had been some bewilderment, and those prosecutors hastily had made some arbitrary decisions.

They had even dismissed the parachutists, and that created a massive problem. Those parachutists were emigrants or agents, who had been dropped above German territory by enemy planes, in order to conduct sabotage and increase the mess. However, the main guilt has to be found among the Gestapo, who arranged that those parachutists have been imprisoned as political prisoners and not political parachutists. Only very few of us really knew who they were. So, naturally, the prosecutors were completely oblivious and set them free.

Only two weeks later, the Peoples' Court in Berlin asked for ten of those parachutists, and I was forced to report that they were gone. General prosecutor Dr. Drescher was arrested and we received the instruction to get hold of them, which of course was only possible to a certain extent. No wonder. Instead of my requested 250 – 300 prisoners, they had released a full number of 700!

After a two days trial, Dr. Drescher was convicted for four months imprisonment. I felt sorry for him, since I was sure that he had not supported the release of so many prisoners.

Meanwhile, our water situation did not improve much, but the fire brigade had at least left us one of their motor fire hoses, so that we could manage the toilet problem quite well for a while. However, we still had to be very economic regarding our use of water. Along with this, an instruction by the Ministry of Justice was aired: Some of the death sentences had to be carried out, against which I rebelled, as I mentioned earlier, so that the convicted were moved to Dreibergen near Bützow, but without those four clergymen that I secretly kept. They had not done anything wrong apart from publicly reading a letter by bishop Graf von Galen addressed to Hitler, in which von Galen blames the Führer for a lot of ongoings.

I knew of the letter's content and I assure you that von Galen did not exaggerate – on the contrary. But whoever read this letter to the public was executed. And again, this shows how true the letter was and how guilt-ridden the regime.

Secretly, I showed the clergymen how they could use their chance to escape when the sirens went off. I have not the faintest idea why they never used this opportunity.

Later, when the executions were resumed in our prison (I was already off duty by then), they were among the victims. What a pity!

When the bomb attacks by the allies moved from Hamburg to Bremen, I was instructed to send 15 of my officers over. I mainly chose political leaders, those "150% Party disciples" of my personnel, but they preferred to stay with the Party and give out food to the citizens. I sent them to Bremen, where it was certainly less comfortable than in the vicinity of their beloved Party.

Naturally, that also boomeranged, in the shape of a written statement with the complaint that I had sent them away, though they would have been of more use here with the Party (whose valuable support they were, allegedly). So, again I had to deal with accusations, such as that I would sabotage Party matters and that I had damaged the reputation of the Party ever since 1933, that I had insulted Hitler, that I had only held the usual muster on Hitler's birthday and then deliberately had left the room – just to state a few of the accusations.

An official of the Reich's Ministry of Justice demanded of me that I resign from my duties immediately. I asked why. He said that it was not necessary to state the reason, according to the Enabling Statute. Consequently, I refused to follow that order without receiving a valid explanation. Then, he said, I would be put in a pending position (also according to the Enabling Statute). I became really angry and we had a verbal argument. The official got so agitated that he told me how sick and tired everybody was of my roughs with the Party. My life, he went on, had hung on a thread ever since 1937 and that thread had already been ragged.

Oho, there we go! Now I really went ape and told him that the Ministry should have been pleased to have a man in Hamburg who dared to oppose the Party. And as a thank you, those spineless Berlin people kicked me – how disgusting!

In the long run, that affair was a lost battle to me and Senior Prosecutor Labriga saw to it, that I took sick leave, so that I could – when the age was appropriate – hand in my resignation myself. In doing so, I would at least still get my salary. In May the following year I was put into retirement. Without the support of Labriga, the president of the district court Dr. Schwarz and Gau Judge Schröck, I would never ever have been able to get out of those terrible waters in one piece. I owe them many thanks for their courage and their decency.

The proceedings against me had already been stopped in April. The resolution stated that the plaintiffs had not acted properly and that there had been made-up denunciations and political pomposity, all which had impeded my duty, if not obstructed. I was described as a German man who would not compromise, as a brave soldier and an impeccable officer who always stood up against such manners. I was said to have put strong measures to my personnel, but the strongest to myself.

So, thanks to the sensible attitude of the Gau Court, I was able to get out of this mess quite leniently.

The party did have some decent people around, however, they could not stand up against the major evil. The new regime (post Nazi era) should have taken that into account. I will get back to this point later.

Forms of egotism are nothing new - they have always been there, even during the Imperial era, but they did not become dangerous. The Nazi regime was the first to combine the mass instinct with egotism and to breed the whole thing in a way that it became a capital crime regarding humanity. Again and again, it was those "little Nazis" that tried to or did bring people like me down, out of sheer egotism and a craving for denunciation. These cowards came from the overall mass, and in this I absolutely include the arrogant police, the Gestapo, the concentration camp guards with their approximately 200.000 men belonging to the skull unions!

The hatred and rejection against the regime secretly grew among the people. Under the given circumstances, it was complete insanity to carry on with the war, but the party shut their eyes and ears. Under the heavy weight of their guilt, they did not want to stop, instead, they wanted to pull the people towards their own, well-deserved fate. And still there was a large number of citizens (mainly women) that were seduced by the words of this comedian and quack, that called himself Führer!

By accident, I was around a Nazi meeting in Hamburg-Winterhude when I heard a Party official giving a statement about the victorious development of the war. It was at a time, when the Atlantic Wall came down and the hostile armies were already in France. (*On 25th of August 1942, Hitler ordered to extend the armed shore positions in West France to a part of the planned Atlantic Wall. Author's comment.*)

And this completely mad tomfool declares that it did not mean anything that the Atlantic Wall was defeated. That was all planned, he rushed to explain, the enemy was meant to proceed far into the country and then be destroyed.

I was left to sigh: Oh my God, can there really be so much nonsense in the world?

Next in line was the terrible winter of 1944/45, in which non-stop air raids took place, attacking Hamburg and other cities. Our airforce was literally history and incapable of any sort of defence. And the front of the allies came closer and closer.

Everything got a lot worse with the tactic of low-flying air raids. As a precaution, I hid my family in our weekend cottage in the Lüneburg Heath, south of Hamburg. I stayed in Hamburg but went over to see them frequently. One day, the train that I was on to bring supplies to my family, was attacked by low-flying airplanes. The train came to a halt and caught fire. In front of us, I saw another train that was already ablaze. In order to save ourselves, we all got out and a wild running about commenced. I could not flee so fast, since I had to help a handicapped lady out of the train. I hid her in a nearby ditch, then ran towards a road.

The low-flyers turned around and I had to throw myself – and the cooking pot I held – onto the ground.

They were flying so low that I could well see their faces. They opened fire onto the civilians that had been trying to hide. By all means: I could not understand this behaviour. Especially in Hamburg, we had a strong liking for the English nation.

The English frequently complained that the German nation permitted to get abused by Hitler for his purposes. Apart from the fact, that this was only valid for a part of the nation, the English will still have to prove that they would not act likewise under the same circumstances. Even Churchill, who was perceived in Germany as a fair and honest politician, saw it exactly this way. Those low-flyers have shown that an English Hitler would have found as many companions as this one in Germany. And with cheap, ethical indignation on the winner's side, nothing is proved at all.

A few days after this attack, the German Reich surrendered unconditionally. Now the thirst for revenge reigned. Understandable, at least on the behalf of those that got damaged by the Nazi regime. However, people who had not been harmed at all, participated in this new development.

All of a sudden, there was an agitation against everything and everyone, no matter whether guilty or not. Every possible sort of evilness started to emerge all around, and it was a well-known fact that most defamations and denunciations occurred on grounds of envy or because one saw a personal advantage coming out of it or simply just out of personal spitefulness!

Those methods were quite similar to those used by the Third Reich: Criminal Acts such as forced shop-closure, seizure of appartments, arrests, prohibiting professions, forced labour, you name it. With this happening, it was no wonder that you could hear the following phrase everywhere: "Dear Lord, give us the fifth Reich. The fourth is just like the third."

If you want to condemn the Nazi regime, you have to do it with a pure heart and not come up with methods that were so similar to the Nazi mentality. After this reign of horror, the German nation needed justice more than anything.

It is one thing to punish criminals, but another thing to pursue citizens whose mere guilt was to believe in a Party that cheated on them anyway.

Naturally, the embitterment concerning the regime was more than justified. But did they improve anything with their deprivation of rights and their spitefulness? No!
Responsible for those senseless actions were mainly the allies, probably. They thought that they served justice by imprisoning as many people as possible without examining whether an offense had been carried out or not. And the enemy got bad advice, of all possible sources, from German people or offices. I reckon, it was the same people that later got involved in the denazification.
Nobody would have said anything against the examination and purging of public offices. Criminals (acting against humanity and others) had to stand trial anyway. But now there was a pursue of innocent Party members and civilians. That was a unique political insensitivity.

I believe that the democracy in Germany would have gotten a good push without the redundant denazification. Innocent Party members would have been powerful supporters for the democratic principles, after their bitter experiences, and if it was only for their shame and annoyance, that they trusted Hitler thoroughly. We would have achieved the awareness, that only a genuine democracy can prevent a repitition of that terrible era.

All these improper measures made a recuparation of the nation impossible, plus, the sense for justice, that was already damaged during the Hitler years, got bruised even more. Now they were breeding a dangerous hate community, and I have a feeling that the denazification did just the opposite: instead of denazifying there was more nazifying. Especially among those "150% Nazi diciples" which were non party members, there were dangerous individuals that came out of the whole affair without being called to account.

Already during the Hitler years, it was that submissiveness of the authorities and administrations that made it way too easy for the Nazis and took their crave for power to a new level. Now we were facing the same submissiveness regarding the military government.

I was just reading in the papers (*1951, author's comment*), that the office and private rooms of the American Chief Commissioner McCloy had been decorated with exceedingly pompous furniture. His desk had been coated with pig leather and carried a monogram worth 1.000 marks. The armchairs were overlaid with furs, the walls were furbished with shantung silk worth 17.000 marks. This financial burden (and tastelessness) was poured onto the poverty-stricken citizens by German authorities.

McCloy, representing a rich nation, was a lot more empathic and had all the pomp removed and substituted by second-hand furniture. This ethical smack in direction to these disgusting lickers was well deserved. Cases like this occurred frequently, and an English General once very rightly said: "The German either jump at your throat or lie at your feet." Even if this is not always the case, the exception proves the rule.

I would like to show an example for how inappropriate those denazifications were. There was a merchant in Hamburg, that I knew, who had applied for a membership in the NSDAP during the Nazi era. He had only been a paying member, without carrying out any official functions, since beforehand, he had been a member of the Masonic Lodge. He himself was a convinced Nazi and would not believe me, even when I described in detail all the horrible ongoings. Apart from that, he was decent and utterly harmless. After the breakdown of the regime he was exceedingly shocked concerning all the evilness.

He had been denazified and got charged with a sum of 10.000 marks. If they had charged him a smaller sum, such as 2.000 – 3.000, he might willingly have paid it as a sacrifice for his credulity. But instead of paying the enormous amount, he filed a complaint which resulted in the decision that the whole charge was dropped. So were was the gain? Only annoyance and the fee for the lawyer.

Cases like these have nothing to do with rationality or even democracy.

It might look as if I try to put the occurrences during the regime era and the ensuing period onto the same level and, even if unintended, mitigate the first. That is not at all my intention, since that had already been thoroughly done by those responsible after 1945. My hatred concerning the terrible Hitler years remains the same, and if I had been the one convicting the criminals, they would not have gotten away that easily, the way it actually partly happened. Albeit I would have included all those denunciants and would have proceeded, strictly obeying law and justice. The German people would have understood that. Then, the atrocities would have stayed vivid in the minds of our nation, and today, we would not have the headache about how we could shake off the S.R.P.

(*The S.R.P. was the 1949 founded Socialistic Reich Party, which saw itself as a sort of successor of the NSDAP and which was prohibited again in 1952 due to their neofascistic attitudes and their antisemitism, author's comment.*)

Honestly, has nobody noticed that there had been opponents amaong the party, which were now snubbed and turned into the enemy? Most of them could not really change anything without being exposed to enormous danger. The whole Nazism was way too primitive as that sacrificing one's life would have made sense. No, you could only stand up against it, if you used the same shrewdness, and whoever got killed then, did it as a victim of human bestiality.

Everyone who knows me, sees it as a miracle that I survived, since my resistance was anything but a whisper, but in word and deed so clear, that whoever surrounded me, constantly begged me not to expose myself to such a big peril. Whenever I got myself into deep trouble, thank the Lord, there had always been people that helped (also among the party), who understood and spoke for me. Unfortuntely, only few of those who carried out the denazifications could tell the difference. Whether it was civil courage or something else, I am forever grateful that I was able to take action, for reasons of humanity and against any resistance until I was forced to go off duty in 1943. However, it was not the Party that removed me, but the Reich Ministry – because they feared the Party!

Now I would like to describe my own denazification, because it fits perfectly into the context.

Cynically speaking, the Nazis themselves had already and utterly denazified me, but it had to be done officially after 1945. At the beginning, nobody stumbled about the fact, that I had been dismissed prematurely, due to my intention to stop the crude hustle of the Gestapo which led to jeopardizing my own life and that of my family. But it would have been so easy: According to the regulations of the military government, proven resistance against the regime was meant to get you an all-clear file promptly. If they had once addressed the authorities, they would soon have known about my deeds. But no, instead, they were more Catholic than the Pope himself.

First, all my pension earnings were stopped and my saving accounts frozen. Then, all of a sudden, they came over to arrest me. I wanted to know the reason and the official, who intended to get hold of me, indicated with his finger in direction to the collapsed houses on the other side of the road. I had supported the regime, he said, which resulted in the collapse of those houses. I replied that I have never heard so much bullshit in my life. I was asking myself where the hell they had dug out this officer, but it was well known by now that in these times, all sorts of questionable individuals had sneaked into authority offices and the likes.
As I mentioned before, a perfect example was the man who became Chief Inspector, though he had been convicted several times already in the past.
Similar situations were taking place at the Housing Department. They even came up with a committee to decide who could keep their flat and who could not. That had not much to do with democracy, but more with aspirations similar to the eastern zone role model.

Either way, I got arrested. Nobody knew why and there was no judicial resolution. Soon I was brought to the Secret Service, but they had no clue either, why I had been arrested. I was led into a cellar vault. Through the barred doors of the lightless, airless dungeon I could see that several people had already been assembled.

In the dungeon, that I was meant to enter, were three individuals: County Court Directer Dr. Paulik, then the Chief editor of the Nazi newspaper "Das Hamburger Tageblatt" Max Baumann, plus a harmless shipyard worker who had worked up to the last day, but had belonged to the general SS (the most harmless one among the SS unions). There were no toilets and the air was nauseating. During the conversations with my inmates, it turned out that, just like me, they had no idea, why they had been arrested.

In the evening, I was taken to the Art Gallery. The following morning I was transferred to the Camp Neuengamme. At the entrance of the former concentration camp, a Union Jack had been raised and a guard was positioned nearby. We were told to take off our caps twelve steps away from the flagpole and to look at the flag. Well, if you asked me, that was somehow over the top, since there is a significant difference whether you honour a flag as a free man or as a prisoner, who gets punished if he does not follow the orders.

Does this agree with democracy that stands for freedom of conscience at all? But, apart from that, the treatment on behalf of the English was absolutely flawless and correct. A few days later, I was interrrogated by an English examining magistrate. He obviously realized that there was no way to get any confession from me, because the following morning I was suddenly released. I never came to know why I had been arrested in the first place, but I do suspect that it had something to do with the new and restructured German administration offices that were acting arbitrary and beyond the instructions of the military regime.

This harassment over, the next followed pronto. The housing department got in touch with me with the intention to seize my flat. However, due to all the previous events, I had expected to be arrested at any time and was well prepared. I had a deal with my landlady that my daughter and my son-in-law were the official owners. I was, on the papers, just the sub-tennant. With this, I could prove that I did not have a flat on my own.

Finally, in August 1946, the evaluation trial came up. The proceedings were short and without any substance. It was declared that I had been a Party member and a Party judge.

And though it was mentioned in the resolution that I had done everything to soften or prevent all the harshness that the Nationalsocialism implied and that my efforts rose to a limit that I drew the hatred of the Party upon myself, they still thought it necessary to recommend a cut on my pension. On top of this, I was secretly classified as category three, which meant I now had a criminal record. I only heard of this a year later, when the trial at the appeals chamber was on, because, naturally, I had filed a complaint. The proceedings resulted in a complete rehabilitation of my persona. And they did emphasize that I had put my life and my freedom at stake in order to support political prisoners. Besides, it was stated that I had carried out my duties with excellent expertise and according to the principles of decency, law and humanity. And this is how my denazification ended on 3rd of December 1947.

In conclusion I would like to express once again that it was not my personal annoyance that led to my criticizing the post war events, but my concern regarding the development of the domestic policies in our nation.

In addition, I wanted to outline how unimportant and partly perishable those things are that humans believe they have to defend with their alleged politics and therefore complicate matters among them. The pointless craving for recognition and arrogance that is connected to that is the root of all evil.

It is hard to combat that evil, but it can be weakened when you realize that decency, leniency and unswerving sense of justice make any human a true human. That has nothing to do with weakness. On the contrary. I believe that whenever you get to a limit regarding those virtues, you are entitled to press your point with relentless energy.

Humane kindness and decency, combined with uncompromising strictness, when needed, have never failed and belong to the big picture of a genuine democracy. With this pattern, there will not be a "thousand year Reich" with an ensuing denazification ever again.

****

Denazification, testifying and affidavits

During the denazification, the British allies invented a scale system from 1 to 5 with the focus on people in high positions. 1 and 2 were serious, and 3 to 5 were the lighter cases.

The recategorization from 3 to 5 enabled Bredow to get his full pension back, as well as the annulment of the ban on his bank savings in December 1947. The reason for the original pension cut was that he had been a member of the Nazi Party before 1933.

Politician John D. Jarks, Dr. Schaedel and Prof. Dr. Callsen (medics) and Dr. von Sauer (court) had been great help with their testifying for Bredow describing his attitude during the NS regime. Dr. Schaedel, Senior Surgeon in the Hamburg prison, emphasizes in his letters how many unjustly executions have been averted singlehandedly and only by Bredow, and that he was very proud of having worked with him. "Bredow had an extreme aversion towards informers", Dr. Schaedel wrote in his letter. "His temperament led to his openly saying what he thought of the regime, calling Hitler a criminal or culprit many times. I often told him to calm down, since I was fearing for his life."

Dr. Schaedel recalled another event, where Bredow would not shy away from speaking his mind. "He held a speech at the prison in Fuhlsbüttel, shortly after the regime took over. He thanked the Senior Officers for their duty and then spoke to the youngsters, who had just started their jobs. He would advise them to stand in for justice and not expect any extra benefits, particularly saying that a decent man will remain a decent man whether he is a member of the Party or not. And a bastard will remain a bastard, no matter how long he would be in the Party."

This speech was, of course, seen as contemptuous and led to a rebuke from the Chancellery of the Führer.

In the original script, Bredow used the word "Schweinehund", which seemed to have been one of his favorite words for Nazi members. I came across that word many times during my research for this book.

His then neighbour in the village of Jesteburg (South of Hamburg) had been asked to testify as well. He described Bredow as the man who would call the regime devilish, bringing doom over the whole country, calling Hitler a criminal of the kind, that the world has never seen before. "Bredow was very lucky that we had no informers in our neighbourhood, otherwise his ending would have been a very bad one."

Vicar B. Behnen, who was on duty in the Hamburg prison since 1928, and whose main task was the spiritual welfare for inmates from 1933 – 1944, would also testify on Bredow's behalf. He remembers priests that had been imprisoned and sentenced to death that Bredow had tried to protect and treated in the best way possible. "It is against any sense of justice that a man like Bredow would suffer disadvantages for political reasons", he wrote in his solemn affirmation on April 1947.

In January 1948, Robert Bredow received a letter from lawyer E.-G. Ruhle, who wrote the following:
"Dear Mr. Bredow,
thank you for your friendly letter. I am very glad that you have been finally assessed to category five. An outcome that I regard as the only correct one. If I was able to contribute to this new assessment by solemn affirmation, I have only done my duty, since I have always known exactly how you thought about the Nazi regime. I felt that I needed to help you, since you yourself have made plenty of bold efforts to help others and save them from the Gestapo.
With the best wishes for the new year, yours sincerely, Ruhle."

Bredow also had to do his favors for others during the denazification period. He was asked many times by lawyers to affirm that a client was "politically clean", in other words testifying whether or not the subject had supported the Nazi regime or was involved in abuse concerning prisoners. Bredow would gladly do so, if justified, but certainly not always and only because the lawyers wished so. He would stick to the truth and not be swayed.

When asked about administration inspector Walter Willnow, he would bring up all the evil that this man had done to him. Without the help of Senior Prosecutor Labriga and Dr. Schwarz, all the accusations made by Willnow would have resulted in the deportation of Bredow, and probably death.

Senior Constable Hermann Brenncke (then on duty in the prison of Bergedorf) was described by Bredow as an evil and dangerous informer. Brenncke had been intriguing and lying which resulted in some people nearly being arrested, if Bredow had not constantly intervened.

However, for Max Lahts, Bredow would not sign an affidavit, since he had enough reasons not to do so. In his manuscripts, Bredow tried to find as many positive aspects as possible for Lahts' personality, such as his good nature and his empathy. However, Lahts had been a very obedient Party member, so he could not let him appear completely innocent and therefore would not testify in Lahts' favour. He would not go along with lawyer Hans Haack, who described Lahts as modest, correct and fair. Bredow had often enough experienced what a shady character Lahts had been. Lahts would tolerate Bredow's loud opposing, but himself, he preferred to stay in the background whenever difficulties arose.

Receiving a positive affidavit was Mr. Ernst Harbeck, a prison ward having served under the direction of Bredow. Though a Party member since 1932, he was diligent, modest and reserved. Unlike many others, Harbeck had never taken advantage of his membership. Bredow recommended to put Harbeck back on duty, since he was completely harmless. Others had been put back on duty, that were a lot less harmless than Harbeck, he concluded.
Similar positive affidavits were written by Bredow for Mr. Wilhelm Jensen, who was a civil servant in his prison, for Mrs. Else Menke, his secretary and for Ary Friedrich Venediger, a young typist.

Bredow was indeed very fond of Hans Lindemann, district Party leader and member of the Nazi Party before 1933. Like Bredow, he fought against the regime and Bredow gladly testified for him, declaring that the category 3 in which he had been classified was completely wrong.

Lindemann knew about Bredow's opposing manners, but never used these to denounce him. On the contrary: He worked even closer with Bredow, who could trust him with his life.

He also testified in favor of Senior District Party Judge (Oberlandesgerichtsrat) Herbert Wolgast, whom he had known as one of the most decent men, nice to work with and fighting the regime to an amount that Bredow had to step in to save Wolgast from severe punishment. Wolgast knew about Bredow's hatred concerning the regime, but has never taken any advantage of that knowledge. Bredow praised him as one of the finest men in that dark era.

Epilogue

Robert Bredow died in 1960 at the age of 82 after a short but serious illness. Sometimes I visit his grave, do a bit of cleaning and plant some flowers. I enjoy doing it, since, after all, I carry his genes. He was one of my ancestors.

Sources:
Forschungsstelle für Zeitgeschichte in Hamburg,
Signatur 12-1_Bredow and
Signatur B_Erinnerungsschreiben (A-Z), 3.
Staatsarchiv Hamburg, 242-7 Strafvollzugakte 139.

Photos:
All photos belong to Phoebe Monk, who has the only copyright.

Thank you!
to the Staatsarchiv Hamburg,
to the Forschungsstelle für Zeitgeschichte Hamburg
to the remand prison in Hamburg, for the support during my
research.